SPEED
MACHINES

Ian Graham
Consultant: John Farndon

Miles Kelly

CONTENTS

◀ The fastest racing motorbikes compete in the MotoGP championship. Using great skill and accuracy, the riders are able to position their bikes only inches from each other at high speed.

RAIL Stars

High-speed trains with a top speed of up to 200 mph (320 km/h), or even faster, whisk passengers from city to city in Europe and the Far East. These sleek, streamlined electric trains run on special tracks so they don't need to slow down for other trains or tight bends.

AGV
FASTEST WHEELED TRAIN IN PASSENGER SERVICE

Years of service: From 2012
Developed in: France
Top speed: 220 mph (360 km/h)
Capacity: Up to 650 passengers
Train length: Up to 820 ft (250 m)

GOING FASTER

The fastest and most modern high-speed trains in Europe are called AGV (Automotrice à Grande Vitesse). Instead of having a power car at each end of the train, an AGV has electric motors under its whole length, making more room inside for passengers. The AGV can go faster than other trains because it has more efficient motors and a more streamlined shape.

TGV
FASTEST WHEELED TRAIN

Years of service: From 1981
Developed in: France
Top speed: 357 mph (574 km/h)
Capacity: 345–750 passengers
Train length: 657–1,293 ft (200–394 m)

AGV TRAINS CAN MAKE A JOURNEY OF 600 MI (1,000 KM) IN ONLY THREE HOURS.

SUPER TGV

French high-speed trains called TGV normally carry passengers at an average speed of 175 mph (280 km/h), but a specially modified TGV set a world-record speed of 357 mph (574 km/h) on April 3, 2007. This is faster than a racing car at full throttle and it's still the world-record speed for any wheeled train.

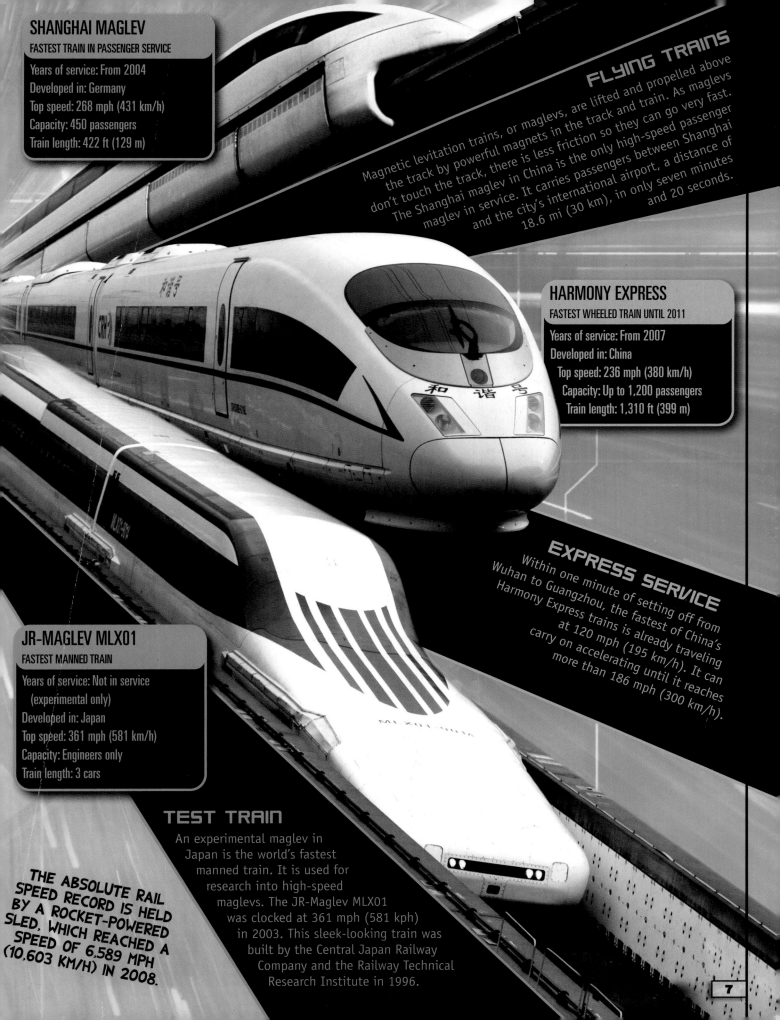

SHANGHAI MAGLEV
FASTEST TRAIN IN PASSENGER SERVICE

Years of service: From 2004
Developed in: Germany
Top speed: 268 mph (431 km/h)
Capacity: 450 passengers
Train length: 422 ft (129 m)

FLYING TRAINS

Magnetic levitation trains, or maglevs, are lifted and propelled above the track by powerful magnets in the track and train. As maglevs don't touch the track, there is less friction so they can go very fast. The Shanghai maglev in China is the only high-speed passenger maglev in service. It carries passengers between Shanghai and the city's international airport, a distance of 18.6 mi (30 km), in only seven minutes and 20 seconds.

HARMONY EXPRESS
FASTEST WHEELED TRAIN UNTIL 2011

Years of service: From 2007
Developed in: China
Top speed: 236 mph (380 km/h)
Capacity: Up to 1,200 passengers
Train length: 1,310 ft (399 m)

EXPRESS SERVICE

Within one minute of setting off from Wuhan to Guangzhou, the fastest of China's Harmony Express trains is already traveling at 120 mph (195 km/h). It can carry on accelerating until it reaches more than 186 mph (300 km/h).

JR-MAGLEV MLX01
FASTEST MANNED TRAIN

Years of service: Not in service (experimental only)
Developed in: Japan
Top speed: 361 mph (581 km/h)
Capacity: Engineers only
Train length: 3 cars

TEST TRAIN

An experimental maglev in Japan is the world's fastest manned train. It is used for research into high-speed maglevs. The JR-Maglev MLX01 was clocked at 361 mph (581 kph) in 2003. This sleek-looking train was built by the Central Japan Railway Company and the Railway Technical Research Institute in 1996.

THE ABSOLUTE RAIL SPEED RECORD IS HELD BY A ROCKET-POWERED SLED, WHICH REACHED A SPEED OF 6,589 MPH (10,603 KM/H) IN 2008.

SUPERSONIC
in the Skies

The fastest military planes in service today are supersonic—they fly faster than the speed of sound. Immensely powerful jet engines boost them to a top speed of more than 1,500 mph (2,400 km/h).

MACH 1

Sound travels faster in warm air than cold air. In warm air near the ground, the speed of sound might be 774 mph (1,246 km/h). In cold air high above the ground, where jet planes fly, the speed of sound might be as low as 660 mph (1,062 km/h). Mach 1 is the speed of something moving through air (or a fluid) compared to the speed of sound. A plane flying at Mach 1 is flying at the speed of sound.

Thundering boom

When a plane reaches the speed of sound, the air in front of it can't move out of the way fast enough. The air piles up in front of the plane and gets squashed into a high-pressure wall called a shock wave. The shock wave spreads out into the surrounding air. If it reaches the ground, you hear it as a bang—a sonic boom—as it sweeps past.

A SHOCK WAVE SPREADS OUT FROM THE NOSE OF A SUPERSONIC AIRCRAFT LIKE A BOAT'S BOW WAVE.

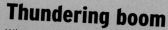

X PLANES SUPERSONIC

X-planes are a series of experimental aircraft built since the 1940s to test new flight technologies. The first problem the X-planes were put to work on was how to fly faster than the speed of sound. It took 50 flights in nearly two years to make the first supersonic flight.

X-1

1947 Chuck Yeager makes history by piloting the rocket-powered X-1 through the sound barrier.

X-5

1951 The X-5 can change the angle of its wings to study its effect on a plane's speed.

MAX SPEED:	MACH 1		MACH 0.95

Roasting reheat

Some fighters are boosted to supersonic speed using reheat—burning extra fuel in the engine exhaust to give the plane an additional push. Reheat is also used to supply more power for takeoff, but it uses up fuel very quickly. Planes such as the F-22 Raptor can fly at supersonic speeds without having to use reheat. This is called supercruise.

◄ Burning extra fuel to go supersonic gives a fighter a fiery trail.

Making clouds

Shock waves are invisible, but sometimes the weather conditions are just right for them to show up. When a supersonic plane hurtles through moist air, a cloud may form behind the shock wave. It's called a vapor cone. Rockets can cause the same effect, so if you see a rocket being launched, watch carefully and you might see a vapor cone forming around it as it soars through the air on its way into space.

► A vapor cone is visible behind this fighter aircraft as it passes through the sound barrier.

▼ The Eurofighter has tiny wings called canards on its nose to enable it to maneuver faster.

Flying ducks

For a supersonic fighter, being able to turn, dive, and climb quickly is just as important as its top speed. Fast maneuvers help a pilot to track a target or to escape from danger quickly. Some fighters have tiny wings called canards (French for "duck") on their nose. Tilting the canards lets the plane perform lightning-fast maneuvers.

X-1A
1953 The X-1A is built to study flight at speeds faster than twice the speed of sound.
MACH 2.4

X-2
1954 The X-2 uses more advanced swept-back wings to try to push its speed faster.
MACH 3.1

X-1E
1955 Based on the X-1, the tiny-winged X-1E is the last of the first X-plane series.
MACH 2.24

AWESOME
Hyperplanes

Aircraft that fly faster than the speed of sound are supersonic, but aircraft that fly faster than five times the speed of sound are *hyper*sonic. Experimental hypersonic aircraft are already being built and tested. A hypersonic airliner would be able to carry passengers from New York, U.S., to Tokyo, Japan, in two hours—a flight that takes about 12 hours today.

▶ Boeing's X-51A is designed to test scramjet engines flying at 3,600 mph (5,800 km/h) or more.

SCRAMJETS

Scramjet engine

Hypersonic aircraft need special engines because ordinary jet engines don't work at such high speeds. They are powered by rockets or jet engines called scramjets. A scramjet engine has no moving parts. Air flows into the engine and is squashed. Then burning fuel makes the air expand and rush out of the engine as a fast jet, propelling the aircraft forward at high speed.

Heat given out

Super boost

On May 26, 2010, an unmanned experimental aircraft called the Boeing X-51A Waverider was dropped from a B-52 bomber. Its rocket engine fired and boosted it to Mach 4.5. Then its scramjet engine started and accelerated it to Mach 5.

◀ Colors are used to show the temperature of the X-43A at Mach 7. Red is the hottest.

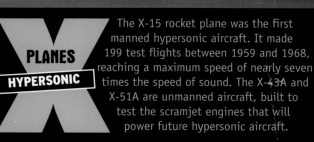

X PLANES HYPERSONIC

The X-15 rocket plane was the first manned hypersonic aircraft. It made 199 test flights between 1959 and 1968, reaching a maximum speed of nearly seven times the speed of sound. The X-43A and X-51A are unmanned aircraft, built to test the scramjet engines that will power future hypersonic aircraft.

1951 The pilotless X-7 was an early testbed for hypersonic engines.

1967 One of the most awesome hyperplanes, the X-15 carried a pilot, propelling Captain William Knight to 4,520 mph (7,275 km/h).

MAX SPEED:	MACH 4.3	MACH 6.7

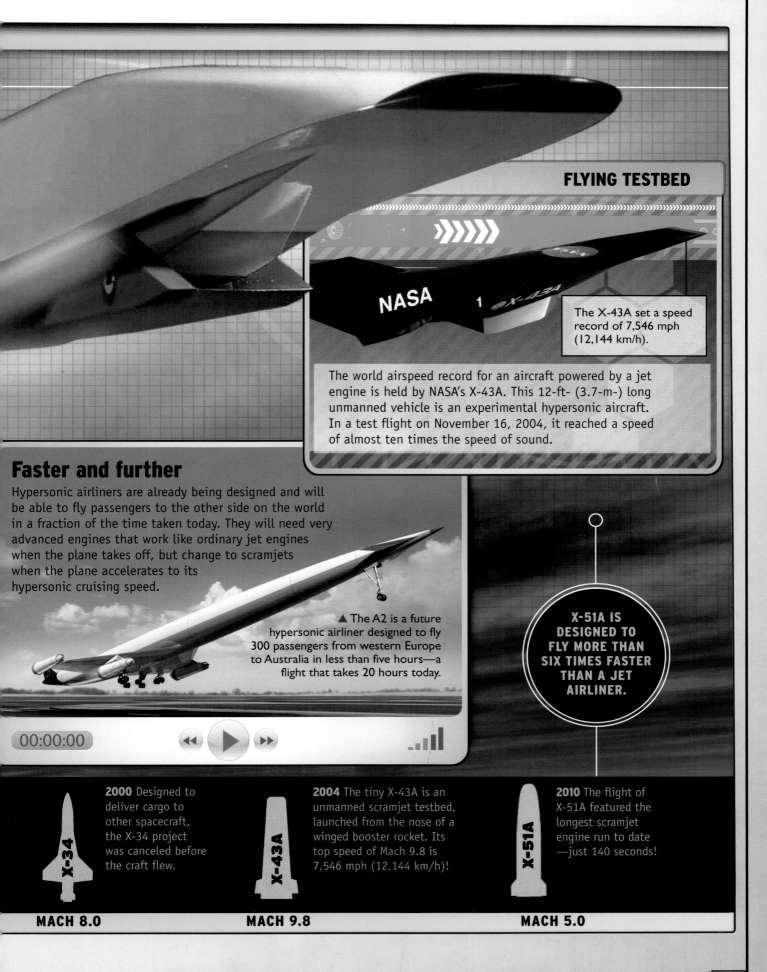

The X-43A set a speed record of 7,546 mph (12,144 km/h).

The world airspeed record for an aircraft powered by a jet engine is held by NASA's X-43A. This 12-ft- (3.7-m-) long unmanned vehicle is an experimental hypersonic aircraft. In a test flight on November 16, 2004, it reached a speed of almost ten times the speed of sound.

Faster and further

Hypersonic airliners are already being designed and will be able to fly passengers to the other side on the world in a fraction of the time taken today. They will need very advanced engines that work like ordinary jet engines when the plane takes off, but change to scramjets when the plane accelerates to its hypersonic cruising speed.

▲ The A2 is a future hypersonic airliner designed to fly 300 passengers from western Europe to Australia in less than five hours—a flight that takes 20 hours today.

00:00:00

X-51A IS DESIGNED TO FLY MORE THAN SIX TIMES FASTER THAN A JET AIRLINER.

2000 Designed to deliver cargo to other spacecraft, the X-34 project was canceled before the craft flew.

X-34

MACH 8.0

2004 The tiny X-43A is an unmanned scramjet testbed, launched from the nose of a winged booster rocket. Its top speed of Mach 9.8 is 7,546 mph (12,144 km/h)!

X-43A

MACH 9.8

2010 The flight of X-51A featured the longest scramjet engine run to date —just 140 seconds!

X-51A

MACH 5.0

Top TAKEOFF

Planes are able to take off only if they move through the air fast enough. An airliner has to accelerate to at least 150 mph (240 km/h) before its wings create enough lift to cause the plane to defy gravity and leave the ground.

▶ Concorde's mighty jet engines powered the plane to a top speed of more than 1,300 mph (2,100 km/h).

The need for speed

The supersonic airliner Concorde had to go much faster than other airliners before it could take off. Its wings were built for flying at twice the speed of sound, so they didn't produce much lift at lower speeds. Concorde had to reach 225 mph (360 km/h) before its slender wings generated enough upward force for takeoff.

▼ A navy pilot prepares to be launched along the deck and into the air by catapult.

Elastic fantastic

An aircraft carrier has a runway, but it isn't long enough for modern fighter jets to reach takeoff speed. Jets have to be hurled along the deck by a powerful catapult so they're going fast enough to fly when they reach the end. The catapult can boost a 47,000-lb (21-ton) plane from zero to 165 mph (265 km/h) in only two seconds.

Air drop

Some of the fastest aircraft can't take off under their own power. Instead, they are carried into the air by another aircraft. SpaceShipOne was a rocket plane carried aloft by an aircraft called White Knight. At a height of 50,000 ft (15,240 m), White Knight dropped SpaceShipOne, which then fired its rocket and soared away. Being launched in the air like this saved weight and enabled SpaceShipOne to fly faster and higher.

▼ White Knight was specially designed to take off with the SpaceShipOne rocket plane hanging beneath it.

White Knight

SpaceShipOne

THE CATAPULTS THAT LAUNCH NAVY PLANES FROM AIRCRAFT CARRIERS ARE POWERED BY HIGH-PRESSURE STEAM.

THE AIRBUS A380 WEIGHS AS MUCH AS 165 ELEPHANTS.

GIANT flyer

The enormous Airbus A380 is the world's biggest airliner. Its massive wings cover enough space to park 140 cars. This huge airliner accelerates to a speed of 170 mph (280 km/h) on the ground before its wings are able lift the 1.25-million-lb (625-ton) aircraft into the air.

▼ The shape and enormous size of the A380 airliner's wings enable it to take off at the same speed as much smaller, lighter planes.

▶ A racing boat can take off if it bounces off a wave and air rushes underneath, pushing it upward.

Keep it down

The fastest cars and boats are sometimes in danger of taking off. In 1983, Richard Noble set a land speed record of 633 mph (1,018 km/h) in his jet-powered car, *Thrust 2*. If he'd gone just 7 mph (11 km/h) faster, *Thrust 2* would have taken off!

Space
SPEEDERS

What goes up must come down... unless it's a spacecraft. Gravity normally pulls everything down to Earth, but if something travels fast enough, it goes into orbit or heads out toward the Moon or planets. The closer an orbiting spacecraft is to Earth, the faster it has to travel to stay in orbit.

Hubble Space Telescope:
Orbital altitude: 347 mi (558 km)
Orbital speed: 16,960 mph (27,290 km/h)

ZOOMING THROUGH SPACE

The fastest manned vehicle ever is the *Apollo 10* command module. This tiny space capsule returned to Earth from the Moon in 1969 with three astronauts onboard. Just before it plunged into Earth's atmosphere and splashed down, it reached a top speed of 24,791 mph (39,897 km/h).

International Space Station
Orbital altitude: 220 mi (354 km)
Orbital speed: 17,220 mph (27,720 km/h)

Space flyer

The International Space Station is gradually slowed down by the thin wisps of atmosphere it flies through, which causes it to lose height. It has to be moved back up to a higher orbit several times a year by firing its own rocket engines or those of a visiting spacecraft.

Eye in the sky

The Hubble Space Telescope has completed one orbit of Earth every 97 minutes since its launch in 1990. From its vantage point above the cloudy atmosphere, Hubble's cameras and other instruments have a clear view of stars and galaxies.

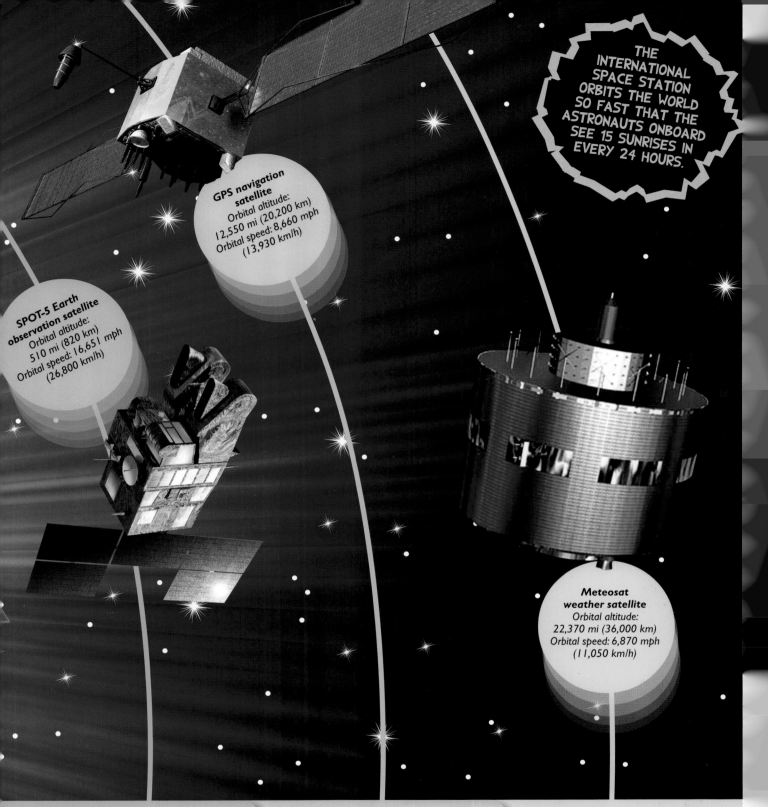

THE INTERNATIONAL SPACE STATION ORBITS THE WORLD SO FAST THAT THE ASTRONAUTS ONBOARD SEE 15 SUNRISES IN EVERY 24 HOURS.

GPS navigation satellite
Orbital altitude:
12,550 mi (20,200 km)
Orbital speed: 8,660 mph
(13,930 km/h)

SPOT-5 Earth observation satellite
Orbital altitude:
510 mi (820 km)
Orbital speed: 16,651 mph
(26,800 km/h)

Meteosat weather satellite
Orbital altitude:
22,370 mi (36,000 km)
Orbital speed: 6,870 mph
(11,050 km/h)

Studying Earth

SPOT-5 is an Earth observation satellite. It circles the world from pole to pole, completing an orbit every 101 minutes as Earth spins beneath it. It passes over each part of the planet every 26 days. Launched in 2002, SPOT-5's photographs are used for town planning, studying land use, terrain modeling, agriculture, monitoring natural disasters, and oil and gas exploration.

Where am I?

GPS (Global Positioning System) satellites help travelers to locate their position and calculate the journey to a specific destination. Their orbit is 60 times higher than the International Space Station. GPS began as a military project to enable U.S. nuclear missile submarines to work out precisely where they were in the ocean.

Watching the weather

Meteosat weather satellites monitor Earth's weather systems. Their orbit above the Equator is chosen so that they take 24 hours to circle Earth. As Earth spins once every 24 hours, too, the satellite appears to hover over the same spot. This is called a geostationary orbit.

STRANGE Sailboats

Yachts that are specially built to win races and set speed records don't look like ordinary boats. They are designed to squeeze every possible bit of power out of the wind—skimming across the top of the water or even flying above it.

IN DECEMBER 2008, AT A SPEED OF 59 MPH (95 KM/H), SAILROCKET 1 TOOK OFF, SOMERSAULTED IN MIDAIR, AND CRASHED INTO THE SEA!

▶ Sailrocket 2 will try to beat the world speed sailing record. Its odd shape is designed so that both the water and wind forces acting on the boat are perfectly balanced.

Rocket boat

One of the strangest-looking, high-speed yachts is a record-breaker called *Sailrocket 2*. Its sail stands on a float to one side of the boat's hull. The sail is rigid, like a plane's wing standing on end. It is perfectly shaped to propel the yacht at high speed in strong winds. The pilot sits in a tiny cockpit at one end of the hull.

▲ The catamaran *Alinghi 5* chases the trimaran *USA-17* in a thrilling dash to the finish line. The masts of these giant racing yachts stand nearly 200 ft (60 m) high.

International Moths are tricky to sail. Sailors use their weight to keep the tiny boats balanced.

Underwater wings

International Moths are small, one-person sailing boats just over 10 ft (3 m) long. Each boat's ultralight hull weighs only 20 lb (10 kg). Like the giant hydrofoil yacht, *Hydroptère*, International Moths have underwater wings. When their hulls rise out of the water—which doubles their speed—they sail along silently. The world record speed for an International Moth is 35.3 mph (56.9 km/h), set by Rob Gough during a training session on May 2, 2010, near Hobart, Tasmania.

Two hulls or three?

Most boats have one hull—the part of the boat that sits in the water. The fastest racing yachts have two or even three hulls. Two or three slender hulls cut through the water faster than one large hull. A two-hulled yacht is called a catamaran and a three-huller is known as a trimaran. In the hands of an expert crew, a racing yacht can reach a top speed of more than 35 mph (55 km/h).

On September 4, 2009, *Hydroptère* set a world record yacht speed of 59 mph (95 km/h).

French flyer

The record-breaking racing yacht *Hydroptère* looks like an ordinary racing yacht until it starts picking up speed. It rises higher and higher until its hull is out of the water altogether. The secret of its amazing performance is a pair of underwater wings called hydrofoils. As they slice through the water, they work like aircraft wings and lift the whole boat. Eventually, only the wings are in the water. As the hull doesn't have to push through the water, *Hydroptère* can reach high speeds.

Power and SPRAY

Powerboats can speed through water as fast as racing cars move on land. All sorts and sizes of powerboats race against each other, from tiny one-person craft to mighty ocean-going vessels. The boats are divided into types, or classes, each with its own design rules. When the starting gun is fired, their spinning propellers turn the water into frothy, white foam as they accelerate to awesome speeds.

Ocean racers

Offshore powerboat racers can plow through the waves at astonishing speeds. Class 1 boats are the fastest. These racing machines are catamarans up to 50 ft (15 m) long and weighing about 5.5 tons (5 tons). Their twin engines can power them through the waves at up to 150 mph (240 km/h).

▶ The super-streamlined hulls of these offshore powerboats slice across the wave tops as they vie for a top position during a thrilling race.

RACING BOATS OFTEN HAVE PROPELLERS AT THE WATER'S SURFACE, CALLED SURFACE-PIERCING PROPELLERS.

MOST BOATS AND SHIPS ARE MOVED THROUGH THE WATER BY PROPELLERS UNDERNEATH THE VESSEL.

WITH ONLY HALF OF EACH PROPELLER UNDERWATER, THEY ENABLE A BOAT TO GO UP TO 30 PERCENT FASTER THAN THOSE WITH UNDERWATER PROPELLERS.

Power planing

Hydroplanes are small, single-engine racing boats that skim across the surface of the water instead of pushing through it. As they speed up, they rise higher until they're sitting on top of the water. This is called planing. When a hydroplane is planing, it touches the water at only three small points—two floats called sponsons at the front and the propeller at the back.

▲ Hydroplanes can exceed 100 mph (160 km/h) and a few have topped 200 mph (320 km/h) on a straight course.

Grand Prix of the Sea

Powerboat Grand Prix of the Sea (GPS) is the fastest-growing type of international powerboat racing. There are two classes of GPS boats—Evolution and Supersport. Evolution boats are specially built for racing. They're about 43 ft (13 m) long and weigh as much as 15,400 lb (7.7 tons). Supersport boats are the same as boats that anyone can buy. All GPS boats are twin-engine monohulls, crewed by at least two people—a pilot who steers the boat and someone who controls the engine power.

EACH OF A CLASS 1 RACING POWERBOAT'S TWO ENGINES IS FOUR OR FIVE TIMES BIGGER THAN A FAMILY CAR ENGINE.

▲ Powerboat GPS racing boats can reach top speeds of 125 mph (200 km/h).

PUSHING the Limit

Sports scientists are constantly looking for ways to make athletes go faster within the rules of their sports. In their quest to win races and set records, they make use of the latest inventions, advances in technology, and cutting-edge materials to push the human body to new limits.

Carbon magic

Cyclists who compete at the highest level ride the most advanced bicycles. Olympic bikes are made of an ultralightweight material called carbon fiber. To save even more weight, there are no brakes or gears, meaning the whole bike can weigh less than 15 lb (7 kg).

▲ High-tech swimsuits enable swimmers, such as American Michael Phelps, to glide through water faster.

A second skin

To increase a swimmer's speed, scientists looked to the animal world for inspiration. Sharks are efficient swimmers because their skin is covered with tiny toothlike points called denticles, making it easier for water to flow round the body. Scientists created swimsuits that mimic shark skin and added elastic panels to streamline the swimmer's body. Of the 25 swimming world records broken at the Beijing Olympics in 2008, 23 were by swimmers wearing these high-tech suits.

THE CARBON FIBER MATERIAL THAT RACING BIKES ARE MADE OF IS UP TO TEN TIMES STRONGER AND FOUR TIMES LIGHTER THAN STEEL.

▲ An Olympic racing bike has spokeless disk wheels to reduce air resistance or drag.

▼ Wearing a pointed helmet cuts the speed-sapping drag caused by a cyclist's head by two percent.

Mad hatters

The pointed helmet worn by a track cyclist gives the rider's head the most aerodynamic shape to go as fast as possible. It reduces air resistance and lets the rider gain a fraction of a second on every lap of the track.

MANUFACTURERS USE THE STRONGEST MATERIALS AND FIBERS TO MAKE RUNNING SHOES SO LIGHT AND THIN THAT THE RUNNER FEELS ALMOST BAREFOOT.

▼ Blades cleverly mimic the action of human legs, even though they have no moving parts or joints.

Bending blades

Using clever technology, disabled athletes can run as fast as the best able-bodied athletes by wearing carbon fiber "legs" called blades. When a runner takes a step, the body's weight bends the blade and the blade stores the energy produced. As the runner lifts his foot to take the next step, the blade springs back and releases its energy, enabling the runner to move quickly.

Speedy Shapes

The wedge-shaped Italdesign Quaranta is a three-seat, 155-mph (250-km/h) prototype of a future road car.

The shape of a racer or record-breaker is as important as its engine power, and is vital for reaching top speed. The wrong shape catches and stirs up the air, slowing down the vehicle. The right shape lets air slide around the vehicle as quickly and easily as possible without slowing it down.

Virtual world

A lot of vehicle testing is done without using models or wind tunnels. Computers are programmed with a vehicle's size and shape. Then the computer calculates how air would flow around the vehicle. This lets designers check new designs quickly without having to wait for models to be made or wind tunnel tests to be carried out.

A supercomputer simulates the way air flows around a new car. Colors are added to show changes in air pressure.

▼ With an ultrasmooth body and a large area of solar cells on top, some solar-powered racing cars can reach a top speed of 75 mph (120 km/h).

Solar speeders

Air resistance eats up engine power, so shape is especially important for cars that have very little driving force. The electric cars that compete in the World Solar Challenge, a 1,860-mi (3,000-km) race across Australia, are powered by sunlight. The cars are covered with solar cells that change light into electricity. Their body shape is carefully designed to cause the least air resistance.

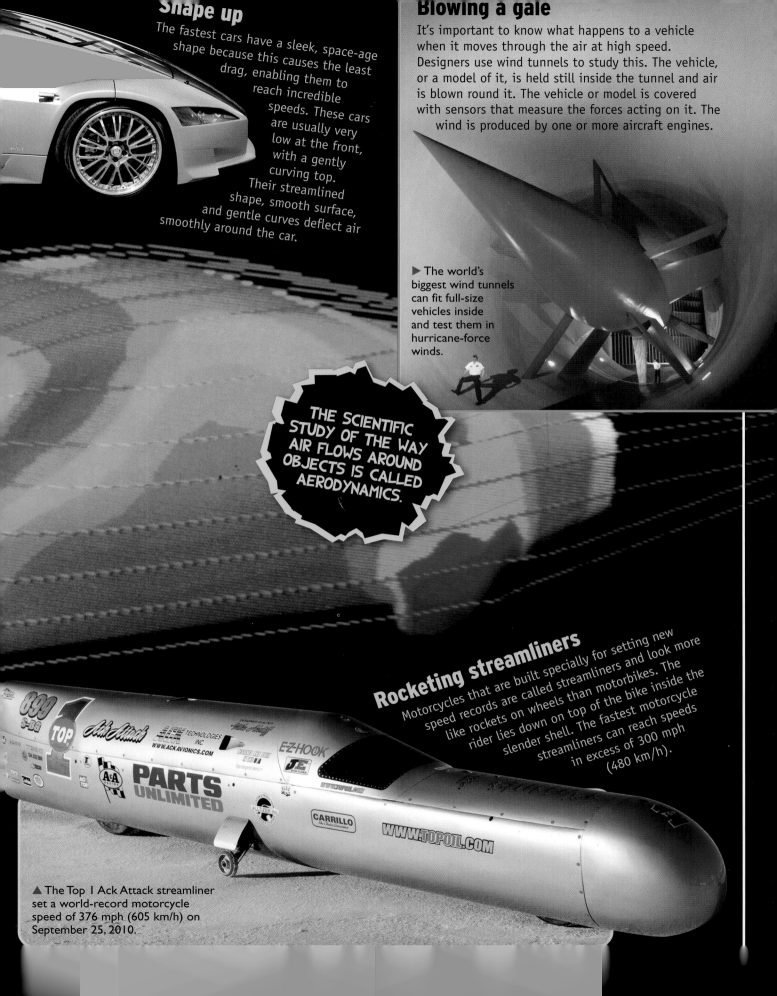

Shape up

The fastest cars have a sleek, space-age shape because this causes the least drag, enabling them to reach incredible speeds. These cars are usually very low at the front, with a gently curving top. Their streamlined shape, smooth surface, and gentle curves deflect air smoothly around the car.

Blowing a gale

It's important to know what happens to a vehicle when it moves through the air at high speed. Designers use wind tunnels to study this. The vehicle, or a model of it, is held still inside the tunnel and air is blown round it. The vehicle or model is covered with sensors that measure the forces acting on it. The wind is produced by one or more aircraft engines.

▶ The world's biggest wind tunnels can fit full-size vehicles inside and test them in hurricane-force winds.

THE SCIENTIFIC STUDY OF THE WAY AIR FLOWS AROUND OBJECTS IS CALLED AERODYNAMICS.

Rocketing streamliners

Motorcycles that are built specially for setting new speed records are called streamliners and look more like rockets on wheels than motorbikes. The rider lies down on top of the bike inside the slender shell. The fastest motorcycle streamliners can reach speeds in excess of 300 mph (480 km/h).

▲ The Top 1 Ack Attack streamliner set a world-record motorcycle speed of 376 mph (605 km/h) on September 25, 2010.

The Right FORMULA

The Formula 1 world championship is the most popular international motorsport in the world. The cars are engineering and design marvels—half the weight of ordinary family cars, but five times more powerful. As they scythe through the air, their "wings" and body shape create a downforce that sticks them to the track, enabling them to corner—fast.

FIRE!

Each car has an automatic fire extinguisher system that sprays foam all over the chassis and engine if a fire breaks out. The drivers also wear fireproof suits, which can protect them from flames as hot as 1,550°F (840°C) for 11 seconds—long enough for help to arrive.

GAME OVER!

‹ SELECT CAR ›

TIRES—designed to last for only one race, or about 185 mi (300 km), compared to more than 25,000 mi (40,000 km) for ordinary car tires

‹ MATERIALS ›

‹ CARBON FIBER ›

Designers make use of the latest materials to produce an F1 car that is light, yet strong. The car's main frame, or chassis, its body, and many of its smaller parts are made of carbon fiber, a material that is up to ten times stronger than steel and a fraction of its weight.

Carbon fiber starts off as a flimsy woven mat, but when soaked in resin, it sets hard.

‹ SELECT ›

FRONT WING— creates one quarter of the car's downforce

DISK BRAKE—slows or stops the car, using carbon fiber disks that can reach a temperature of 2,200°F (1,200°C)

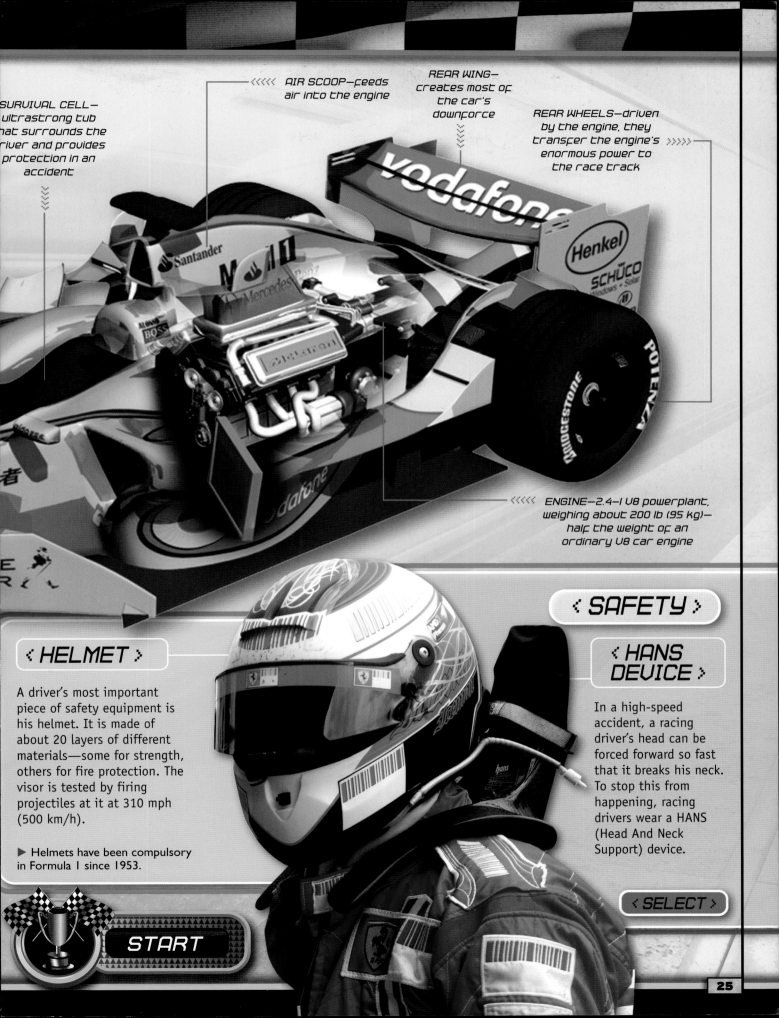

SURVIVAL CELL—
ultrastrong tub
that surrounds the
driver and provides
protection in an
accident

AIR SCOOP—feeds
air into the engine

REAR WING—
creates most of
the car's
downforce

REAR WHEELS—driven
by the engine, they
transfer the engine's
enormous power to
the race track

ENGINE—2.4-l V8 powerplant,
weighing about 200 lb (95 kg)—
half the weight of an
ordinary V8 car engine

< SAFETY >

< HELMET >

A driver's most important
piece of safety equipment is
his helmet. It is made of
about 20 layers of different
materials—some for strength,
others for fire protection. The
visor is tested by firing
projectiles at it at 310 mph
(500 km/h).

▶ Helmets have been compulsory
in Formula 1 since 1953.

< HANS
DEVICE >

In a high-speed
accident, a racing
driver's head can be
forced forward so fast
that it breaks his neck.
To stop this from
happening, racing
drivers wear a HANS
(Head And Neck
Support) device.

< SELECT >

START

SLEEK Supercars

Fast, powerful, expensive—supercars combine blistering performance with space-age styling. Not only are they as low-slung and streamlined as a racing car, they also have the acceleration to match. Supercars are made only in small numbers by manufacturers including Ferrari, Lamborghini, Porsche, Koenigsegg, Pagani, and Bugatti.

DODGE VIPER

The first thing to notice about a Dodge Viper is its long hood. It covers a massive 8.4-l engine, giving this American supercar a top speed of more than 200 mph (320 km/h). The ten-cylinder engine was developed from a truck engine, but modified to make it lighter and more powerful for use in a sports car.

ENGINE
8.4-l V10;
600 horsepower

0–60 MPH
3.9 sec

TOP SPEED
202 mph (325 km/h)

PRICE
$91,955 (£56,595)

ENZO FERRARI

This Italian car manufacturer has been producing some of the world's fastest racing cars and most desirable sports cars for more than 50 years. The Enzo Ferrari supercar was designed and built using technology from Ferrari's Formula 1 racing cars. All 349 Enzo Ferrari supercars were sold before they were even made. Later, another 51 cars were built to bring the total production to 400 cars. The 400th car was auctioned for charity.

ENGINE
6.0-l V12;
660 horsepower

0–60 MPH
3.65 sec

TOP SPEED
217 mph (350 km/h)

PRICE
$1 million
(£615,400)

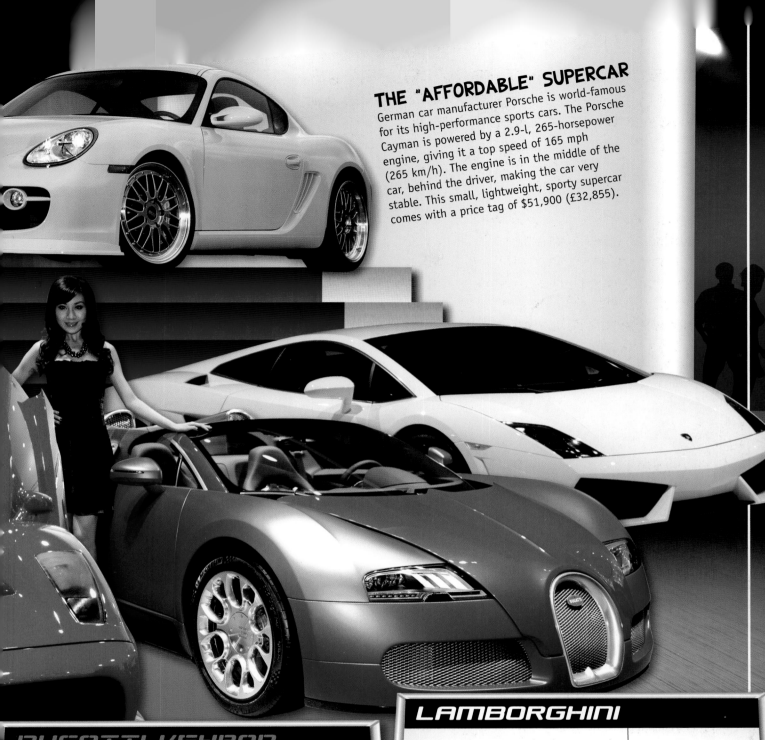

THE "AFFORDABLE" SUPERCAR

German car manufacturer Porsche is world-famous for its high-performance sports cars. The Porsche Cayman is powered by a 2.9-l, 265-horsepower engine, giving it a top speed of 165 mph (265 km/h). The engine is in the middle of the car, behind the driver, making the car very stable. This small, lightweight, sporty supercar comes with a price tag of $51,900 (£32,855).

BUGATTI VEYRON

The Bugatti Veyron is the world's fastest production car. The Super Sport model set a world-record speed of 268 mph (431 km/h) on July 3, 2010. Designed for high-speed driving, when it reaches 140 mph (220 km/h), the Veyron automatically lowers itself closer to the ground. At the same time, a wing and spoiler pop up at the back of the car. Air flowing over them help to hold the car down on the road.

ENGINE
8.0-l W16;
1,200 horsepower

0–60 MPH
2.5 sec

TOP SPEED
258 mph
(415 km/h)

PRICE
$2.4 million
(£1.5 million)

LAMBORGHINI

Most cars have two wheels powered by the engine, but all four of the Lamborghini Gallardo's wheels are powered to give improved grip and control. To save weight, the Gallardo's body is made of aluminum instead of steel. Large air intakes under its nose help to keep the powerful mid-mounted engine cool.

ENGINE
5.2-l V10;
560 horsepower

0–60 MPH
3.7 sec

TOP SPEED
202 mph (325 km/h)

PRICE
$220,000 (£139,000)

A race between different cars, bikes, boats, and planes—which would win? Would it be the fastest car, the most powerful dragster, or the most maneuverable motorbike? Or would a plane or boat cross the finish line first? Which would be the Ultimate Winner?

ULTIMATE RACE

SPEED MACHINES

NASCAR

NASCAR racing cars look like souped-up production cars, but are individually handbuilt for racing on road circuits and racing ovals.

Top Speed	200 mph (320 km/h)
Acceleration	Very good
Power	800 hp
Endurance	500 mi (805 km/h)
Maneuverability	Moderate

RED BULL RACING PLANE

The aircraft that take part in the Red Bull Air Race World Championship are small, lightweight, highly maneuverable planes designed for aerobatics and racing.

Top Speed	265 mph (426 km/h)
Acceleration	Good
Power	350 hp
Endurance	477 mi (767 km)
Maneuverability	Good

SUPERBIKE

Superbikes are modified production motorcycles, chosen so that fans of the sport can see bikes similar to their own competing on the race track.

Top Speed	205 mph (330 km/h)
Acceleration	Excellent
Power	215 hp
Endurance	68 mi (110 km)
Maneuverability	Excellent

MOTOGP MOTORCYCLE

MotoGP is the leading international motorcycle championship. The bikes are prototypes, more powerful than many cars but just a fraction of a car's weight.

Top Speed	220 mph (350 km/h)
Acceleration	Excellent
Power	240 hp
Endurance	75 mi (120 km)
Maneuverability	Excellent

TOP FUEL DRAGSTER

These extraordinary cars are designed to achieve the maximum acceleration in a straight line. They have minimal steering, which is used only to make small adjustments in direction.

Top Speed	330 mph (530 km/h)
Acceleration	Excellent
Power	7,000 hp
Endurance	0.25 mi (402 m)
Maneuverability	Almost none

FORMULA 1 RACING CAR

F1 cars are specially designed for racing on circuits with left and right turns. Downforce generated by their body and wings enables them to corner at very high speeds.

Top Speed	225 mph (360 km/h)
Acceleration	Excellent
Power	720 hp
Endurance	200 mi (320 km)
Maneuverability	Excellent

GPS RACING POWERBOAT

These racing prototypes and production boats are slender monohulls powered by two engines. The Evolution class prototypes are the fastest of the GPS boats.

Top Speed	125 mph (200 km/h)
Acceleration	Good
Power	725 hp
Endurance	100 mi (160 km)
Maneuverability	Moderate

INDYCAR

IndyCars are a little faster than F1 cars in a straight line, but F1 cars are able to generate more downforce, so they are faster in turns.

Top Speed	240 mph (385 km/h)
Acceleration	Excellent
Power	650 hp
Endurance	500 mi (805 km)
Maneuverability	Good

UNLIMITED HYDROPLANE

These small boats, powered by helicopter engines, reach breathtaking speeds by skating across the top of the water instead of plowing through it.

Top Speed	200 mph (320 km/h)
Acceleration	Good
Power	3,000 hp
Endurance	12.5 mi (20 km)
Maneuverability	Good

** WINNERS **

Top Speed	Top Fuel Dragster
Acceleration	Top Fuel Dragster
Power	Top Fuel Dragster
Endurance	NASCAR
Maneuverability	Formula 1 racing car

ULTIMATE RACE WINNER:
Formula 1 racing car

Although Top Fuel Dragsters have the best speed, acceleration, and power, F1 cars have the edge with their combination of speed, agility, and endurance. Dragsters can only go in a straight line for 0.25 mi (0.4 km), lasting less than ten seconds. An F1 car can go for hours on a winding track with right and left bends. If you raced a dragster against an F1 car, the dragster would be in the lead at the first corner, then it would either fall over when it tried to turn or it would run out of fuel!

HOT Stuff

Speed and heat go together. When something travels through air very fast, it heats up. The fastest vehicles heat up so much that they would melt if they weren't protected. Airliners that fly up to about twice the speed of sound are made of aluminum. Faster aircraft are made of materials such as titanium that can withstand higher temperatures. Spacecraft that travel even faster need heat shields to protect them.

Shuttle tiles

A heat shield that slowly burns away can be used only once. A different type of heat shield that could be used again and again was developed for the Space Shuttle Orbiter. The hottest parts of the Orbiter reached a temperature of nearly 3,000°F (1,650°C) during reentry— at about 17,000 mph (27,340 km/h) or Mach 25. To protect its aluminum structure, it was covered with heat-resistant tiles and blankets.

▼ The Space Shuttle Orbiter is covered with more than 24,000 tiles. No two tiles are alike—each has a unique shape.

What a scorcher!

When a manned spacecraft reenters Earth's atmosphere, it heats up so much that it becomes a fireball. One way to stop it from melting is to cover the front with a heat shield. The material in an "ablative" heat shield slowly smolders, rather than setting on fire. The new Orion American manned spacecraft currently under construction will use an ablative heat shield to deal with reentry temperatures as high as 5,000°F (2,760°C).

◄ An engineer inspects an Orion spacecraft's heat shield. When this spacecraft returns from the Moon, it will hit Earth's atmosphere at 25,000 mph (40,000 km/h).

The Mars Polar lander's heat shield glows due to friction from Mars' atmosphere.

Landing on Mars

A spacecraft landing on Mars needs a heat shield to save it from burning up as it plunges into the Martian atmosphere. A spacecraft enters the atmosphere at about 12,000 mph (19,300 km/h). The thin atmosphere slows it down and heats it up. Within four minutes, its speed has dropped to 1,000 mph (1,600 km/h) and its heat shield is glowing red-hot. The heat shield has done its job and falls away, leaving the spacecraft to land by parachute.

THE HEAT SHIELD OF A SPACECRAFT ENTERING THE MARTIAN ATMOSPHERE IS HOT ENOUGH TO MELT GOLD.

Space Shuttle tiles were such good insulators that even when they were glowing red-hot in the middle, they could be held safely in the hand.

Cool design

The material chosen for the Space Shuttle's heat shield tiles is an incredibly good insulator. About six percent of it is made of silica, and the rest is air. Heat travels through it very, very slowly. However, the material is very brittle and easily damaged. The Space Shuttle wasn't launched when it was raining, because raindrops could damage the tiles!

SPEEDING
UP

Some vehicles accelerate a lot faster than others. One measurement of acceleration is the time a vehicle takes to go from 0 to 60 mph (100 km/h). A family car takes about ten seconds. The jet-propelled land speed record car, *Thrust SSC*, took 2.5 seconds. Dragsters are even faster and reach 60 mph (100 km/h) in less than one second!

Blistering speed

Great acceleration is vital in motor-racing. The car with the best acceleration gets away from the start line first and reaches the first turn in the lead. Formula 1 and IndyCars can go from 0 to 60 mph (100 km/h) in just over two seconds, or about five times faster than a family car.

▲ At full power, a Formula 1 racing car's engine sucks in an amazing 120 gal (450 l) of air every second.

In a flash

The world's fastest pick-up truck, *Flash Fire*, is powered by a 12,000-hp jet engine from a navy plane. The engine thrusts the truck to 60 mph (100 km/h) in just over one second and boosts it to a top speed of 375 mph (603 km/h).

▶ *Flash Fire*'s jet engine gets through 60 gal (227 l) of fuel in just ten minutes.

Drag speed

Dragsters accelerate faster than any other car. When the driver of a Top Fuel dragster gets the green light, the car goes from 0 to 60 mph (100 km/h) in half a second. Even faster, a rocket-propelled dragster does this in only one fifth of a second!

Smoke pours from the spinning wheels of a dragster at the beginning of a race.

Dr. John Stapp studied the effects of g-force on the human body in the 1940s and '50s by strapping himself to a rocket sled.

Like a bullet

A handful of street-legal motorbikes can accelerate from 0 to 60 mph (100 km/h) in only 2.5 seconds—almost as fast as a F1 car or IndyCar. The fastest street-legal cars are more than seven times heavier than a motorbike, but they're also more than seven times as powerful, so they too can accelerate from 0 to 60 mph (100 km/h) in about 2.5 seconds.

▼ The Suzuki Hayabusa motorbike accelerates as fast as a racing bike.

AWESOME G-FORCE

People traveling in an accelerating vehicle feel a force acting on them called g-force. The faster the acceleration, the stronger the g-force. Stopping suddenly produces g-force, too. The force of gravity pulling you down to the ground is 1 g. An astronaut feels a force of about 3 g during a launch. A force of 50 g or more is usually fatal, but F1 driver David Purley experienced a momentary force of 180 g during a crash—and survived.

Record BREAKERS

Through history, different types of speed machines have become faster by small amounts as people attempt to develop vehicles that can outdo any previous models. Improvements in performance are usually due to inventions or developments, such as a new engine.

To set an official airspeed record, planes must have air-breathing engines and take off and land under their own power.

▼ The Blackbird spy-plane could fly at more than three times the speed of sound.

AIR

SPEED RECORD

In 1906, only three years after the first plane flew, Alberto Santos-Dumont set the first official airspeed record—25.6 mph (41.3 km/h). As flimsy biplanes were replaced by all-metal monoplanes, and propellers gave way to jet engines, the record rose steadily. The last record was set in 1976 by U.S. Air Force Captain Eldon W. Joersz and Major George T. Morgan flying a Lockheed SR-71 Blackbird spy-plane—2,193 mph (3,529 km/h).

2,193 MPH (3,529 KM/H)

LAND

SPEED RECORD

763 MPH (1,228 KM/H)

The first land speed record was set in 1898 by Frenchman Count Gaston de Chasseloup-Laubat in an electric car. He drove the fastest car in the world at 39 mph (63 km/h). The most famous land speed record cars were the Bluebird cars driven by Malcolm Campbell and, later, his son Donald. In the 1960s, Craig Breedlove set a series of land speed records in cars powered by jet engines. In 1997, a jet-car called *Thrust SSC* driven by Royal Air Force fighter pilot Andy Green set a record of 763 mph (1,228 km/h).

Thrust SSC, powered by two jet-fighter engines, is the first car to set a supersonic land speed record.

BRITISH DRIVER MALCOLM CAMPBELL SET MORE LAND SPEED RECORDS THAN ANYONE ELSE—NINE IN 11 YEARS.

MALCOLM CAMPBELL'S SON, DONALD, IS THE ONLY PERSON EVER TO SET NEW LAND SPEED AND WATER SPEED RECORDS IN THE SAME YEAR—1964.

The current water speed record was set by Ken Warby in a jet-powered boat called *Spirit of Australia* that he designed and built himself. On November 20, 1977, he set off across the Blowering Dam lake in Australia and recorded a speed of 288 mph (464 km/h). He returned to Blowering Dam the next year and raised the record to 317 mph (511 km/h).

WATER
SPEED RECORD
317 MPH (511 KM/H)

▲ Donald Campbell set seven world water speed records in *Bluebird K7* between 1955 and 1964.

▼ *Spirit of Australia* was powered by a 6,000-hp Westinghouse J34 jet engine from a fighter plane.

Number CRUNCHERS

The biggest supercomputers work as fast as a billion people each doing a million calculations every second!

Supercomputers are the world's fastest computers. They tackle the most difficult problems that need huge numbers of calculations done very quickly—only a supercomputer can do the trillions upon trillions of calculations needed to show what happens when two black holes collide with each other in space.

The Swiss Federal Institute of Technology is kept warm in winter by water heated by its Aquasar supercomputer.

The first supercomputer was the CDC 6600, built in 1964. It could do a million calculations in one second. The fastest supercomputers today are about 10,000 million times faster.

The speed of the fastest supercomputers is measured in units called petaflops—a petaflop is a thousand trillion calculations per second. A trillion is a million million.

Computer technology advances so quickly that a desktop PC today is as powerful as a supercomputer was ten years ago.

More than half of the world's top 500 supercomputers are in the U.S.

Every six months, in June and November, a list of the world's 500 fastest computers is published. It's called the TOP500.

In October 2010, China's Tianhe-1A supercomputer became the world's fastest computer with a speed of 2.5 petaflops, or 2,500 trillion calculations per second.

Germany's Jugene supercomputer works faster than 50,000 PCs. Its circuit boards fill 72 fridge-sized cabinets.

▼ When Jugene was built in 2007, it was the world's second fastest computer.

Tianhe-1A has the computing power of 175,000 laptops and uses as much electricity as 4,000 homes.

Supercomputers have **doubled** in speed roughly every 14 months since 1993.

Most personal computers use the Microsoft Windows operating system, but nearly all of the world's supercomputers use an operating system called Linux.

In 1996, IBM's Deep Blue became the first supercomputer to **win a chess match** against a world champion chess player, Gary Kasparov.

Supercomputers are able to work so amazingly fast because they have tens of thousands of processors all working at the same time on different parts of a problem—called parallel computing.

Supercomputers are growing in speed and complexity so fast that some scientists think they may become **more intelligent than humans** by about the year 2045.

Supercomputers have to be cooled or they would get hot enough to fry their circuits.

New supercomputers are being built all the time. In June, 2011, a Japanese supercomputer called the K computer reached a speed of **8 petaflops** in tests—more than three times faster than Tianhe-1A.

TOP 10 FASTEST SUPERCOMPUTERS

	SUPERCOMPUTER	SPEED*	COUNTRY
1	K	8.162	Japan
2	Tianhe-1A	2.566	China
3	Jaguar	1.759	U.S.
4	Nebulae	1.271	China
5	TSUBAME 2.0	1.192	Japan
6	Cielo	1.110	U.S.
7	Pleiades	1.088	U.S.
8	Hopper	1.054	U.S.
9	Tera 100	1.050	France
10	Roadrunner	1.042	U.S.

* petaflops (thousand million million calculations per second)

The Earth Simulator was a supercomputer built in Japan by NEC in 2002 to study the global climate and climate change. It was the world's fastest supercomputer until 2004.

IBM is building a supercomputer called Sequoia with a computing speed of 20 petaflops—20,000 trillion calculations per second.

▲ Two boosters strapped to the sides of an *Atlas V* give the rocket extra power and speed.

Liftoff

The fastest ever rocket to leave Earth is an *Atlas V* that carried the New Horizons space probe on its way to the dwarf planet Pluto. Launched in 2006, it reached a speed of 32,256 mph (51,911 km/h) as it sped away from Earth. The spacecraft was as far away as the Moon in only nine hours.

High rise

Dubai's Burj Khalifa skyscraper is the world's tallest building at 2,717 ft (828 m) high. Its elevators set a new record as the world's fastest in 2010. They whisk people up and down the giant building at up to 40 mph (64 km/h).

IN 1955, THE FIRST ELEVATOR TO HOLD THE TITLE OF THE WORLD'S FASTEST MOVED AT 16 MPH (25.6 KM/H).

High-speed elevators reach the top of Burj Khalifa in less than 60 seconds.

GOING UP

If you want to go straight upward as fast as possible, there are lots of ways to choose. You could launch yourself on top of a rocket, zoom up a skyscraper in a high-speed elevator, take a flight in a helicopter, or even hitch a ride on a jet-propelled bedstead!

Space elevator

In the future, you might be able to get to space by taking a ride in an elevator. A cable would extend from the ground to a spacecraft in orbit and an elevator car would climb up the cable to space.

▲ A space elevator would be at least 22,370 mi (36,000 km) tall!

Super chopper

Helicopters can take off straight upward. The fastest helicopter ever built is the Sikorsky X2. A propeller in its tail gives it a top speed of 290 mph (460 km/h). Lessons learned from this experimental super chopper are being used to develop a new high-speed military helicopter.

▲ Sikorsky X2 has two rotors that spin in opposite directions.

Flying bedstead

Apollo astronauts practised landing on the Moon before they did it for real by flying a strange aircraft called the flying bedstead. In the middle, it had a jet engine pointing straight downward.

◀ The flying bedstead was steered by rocket thrusters.

Jet man

How would you like to strap a rocket to your back? In a jetpack, hydrogen peroxide fuel in a tank on the pilot's back is converted into steam. The steam takes up more space than the liquid fuel, so it jets out of two pipes that point downward. The jets push the pilot up into the air. The pilot steers by swiveling the jet pipes.

▼ The pilot can only carry enough fuel for flights of 20–30 seconds.

INDEX

Entries in **bold** refer to main subject entries; entries in *italics* refer to illustrations.